I0233166

Necessary

Adjustments

Necessary Adjustments

Khalid Bey

CREATIVE RESEARCH SOCIETY

DEYEL PUBLISHING COMPANY
217 WEST KENNEDY STREET,
SYRACUSE, NEW YORK [13205]

ISBN: 978-0615782973

Printed 2013

For information: https://www.facebook.com/deyelbooks?ref=hl

Cover illustration by Khalid El Bey

Published by

DEYEL PUBLISHING

217 West Kennedy Street, Syracuse, New York [13205]

CREATIVE RESEARCH SOCIETY

Syracuse New York

Printed in the United States of America.

Other Books by the Author

The Key to Character

The African American Dilemma

Now

From My Eyes; Community Memoirs

Love Under Will

The Longest Chord

Other Books Published by Deyel

Sol Azure

Table of Contents

Chapter

Necessary

Adjustments

Dedication

I would like to dedicate this book to many of you throughout our nation who have grown frustrated with government, and I would like to assure each of you that your energy is needed in the cause to make our government(s) better.

It is my sincere hope that elected officials and business persons alike "see the logic" and work together to raise our cities, states and our nation back to point where we are fiscally responsible, socially and culturally empathetic, and efficient in the distribution of services to those whom we are to represent.

Preface

As a voting constituent I have always had my issues with government and its distribution of services. I often felt as if my community was forgotten or neglected by the persons whom we chose to speak on our behalf. Most of the people, who live in the community where I live, felt or still think or feel the same way.

Once I began working for government, and certainly once I became an elected official myself, I learned that a lot of what I and others assumed was true; but there was also a lot that I and others did not or do not understand. The need for government education for the constituent and for other reasons that I will mention later have led me to consider sharing my opinion about government and constituent relations.

Before going any further into this discussion, I would like to acknowledge my family, particularly my children, for they are forever my inspiration.

I would like to thank the voters of the City of Syracuse for allowing me the opportunity to work on their behalf and for having faith in my ability to deliver for them. For those who might not have been in my support, I hope that I have or will earn your confidence and support.

I would like to thank my former co-workers in the New York State Senate, amongst whom I learned so much about government and the importance of being responsive to constituents.

Lastly, I would also like to thank many of you, the readers, where ever you are for your positive feedback, expressed appreciation and continued support for what I have to offer.

Sincerely,

-Khalid Bey

Introduction

Over the years, the representatives at the various levels of government, as well as the constituents who actively participate in government on a daily bases has done so from such extreme positions that conflict has become a popular characteristic of government and politics; and this conflict has alienated the general populace. The behavior and the ideas expressed by some of the aforementioned has created such a distaste for government and politics that even a large number of registered voters refuse to be bothered with what has been deemed by many an absolute joke. Politicians are viewed as shysters and government as the untrustworthy, over-bearing "Big Brother" who essentially wastes the time, energy and money of the People. The idea of a politician and the reputation of politicians, in general have become so unattractive, that newly elected persons seldom stand a chance with constituents. Government at every level is often accused of being corrupt, dishonest and lacking in transparency. In so many ways our government representatives have "dropped the ball" and have forgotten about "the People" whom they are to represent; and there are some who have **never** been sincere about improving the conditions of the People to begin with. The politician's preoccupation with his own agenda has caused him to neglect the very reason for which he claimed to have sought public office.

Today there exist a noticeable separation between government and the people that government is intended to serve. What has become an indifference to government on the part of the constituent and inadequate services on the part of government has resulted in the above-mentioned separation. It is my awareness of this troublesome separation and a dire need to re-acclimate the People to government that has caused me to pen this book.

The foundation of the opinions and understanding expressed herein lies in my personal observations and experiences. I am in no way qualifying myself as an expert, but instead an eternal student whose interest is in only determining practical solution(s) for assuring a more responsive, effective and efficient government. This is "just my opinion", and so does not have to be considered by anyone. This book provides an explanation in a way that is clear and easy to comprehend, so that no matter the level of participation in politics and government, the reader could or should understand. In preparing this book I have made every effort to make the reader's experience short and sweet, but impactful. If you the reader find this composition to be even a slight bit enlightening, this book will have served its purpose.

-Khalid Bey

Author

1   Darwinism

The principle idea communicated in Darwinism or Natural Selection is that an organism possessing the ability to adapt to the ever changing environment is an organism that will survive (said changes). To the contrary, an organism that fails to adapt to the changing environment will parish. Darwinism is the source of the ever so popular "survival of the fittest ideal"; an ideal which is obviously so characteristic of our society's political and capitalistic structure. My reason for mentioning Natural Selection will become clear very shortly.

In politics there exists a fundamental difference in the thinking of those occupying the right and those occupying the left. These differences have been the cause of debates for decades. While most of us are familiar with the differing philosophies, I will reiterate as much for the purpose(s) of this book. In consideration of those who may not be political zealots I will clarify who "the right" and "the left" are. I ask that the more politically savvy please forgive me for, and to be patient with, my articulation of what might be elementary to you.

The Right

Persons who are registered in the Republican, Tea, Libertarian and Conservative Parties are commonly referred to as "right-winged". Self determinism lies at the core of the philosophy of those on the right. In our society the constitutional right to free enterprise empowers every individual with the freedom to pursue business or work opportunities that could lead to whatever said individual deems to be satisfying quality of life. This "ideal freedom" is one of the driving forces behind the Republican, Tea Party, Libertarian and Conservative position: that our great nation empowers every man with opportunities for life and liberty in the pursuit of happiness; and so every man is responsible for his own destiny. It is the position of the right that too much government regulation is bad for business and therefore bad for our national economy. Right-winged conservatives as a result endeavor to elect persons of like mind to political office, with the hopes that their preference for smaller government, amongst other things, would be realized. Smaller government or deregulation implies fewer restrictions on business markets and/or corporations and their business operations. Ideally, fewer restrictions on businesses means fewer cost associated with regulations and the sustaining or potential improvement of a business' bottom line.

The Left

Group thinking or selflessness tends to be the philosophy of left. Understanding that no man is an island, it is the position of the Democrats, Working Families Party, liberals, etc. that we must care for our fellow man and that it is the responsibility of government to ensure that the rights and privileges of the People are protected. It is further the position of the left that government regulation is necessary to prevent private industry from establishing monopolies within the various business markets; and to also prevent business from taking advantage of workers and consumers. The recent mortgage crisis is an example of how businesses have and/or can take advantage of its consumers. Relative to Darwinism, it is the organism that fails to adapt to the ever-changing environment and the struggling middle class worker that the left (primarily) expresses compassion for; and this is a very noble effort. Social services, public education, and healthcare (Medicaid / Medicare) are examples of the types of public programs supported by the left. Programs such as these were established for persons who otherwise may not possess the financial, mental, or physical capability to manage the costs associated with the above mentioned services, had these services been provided by private companies, only.

On the right you have the *individual survival dynamic* versus the left's *group survival dynamic*.

Persons on the right and the left, particularly elected persons continue to struggle in their effort(s) to determine a solution for the ever-growing economic problems within our society. Persons on the right say that our great country allows for the individual to be prosperous and that it is the responsibility of the individual to assure that he and his family is provided for. Persons on the left agree with this notion, but adds that compassion should be had for individuals who struggle to achieve the American dream.

On either side of the isle there are some who consider members of the opposite side weak in their understanding and ability as it relates to governing.

There are many who argue against Darwinism for what became a tool which was used in a very popular effort to deem one ethnic group to be genetically inferior to another; or to further clarify, Natural Selection suggests that throughout the evolutionary process there will arise 'new species' of germ(s) considered to be stronger or superior to germs that were incapable of transmutation.[1] While the debate over genetics continue to fade, the general principle regarding the need for an ability to adapt to evolving circumstances, in my opinion, cannot be denied. Society, like life, continually demands an adjustment on the part of the individual. When an individual struggles to 'improve' in accordance with the changing environment or circumstances, the ability for forward progress is disturbed. Often times, inertia or slowed activity is the result. If a cell within the body or even an atom stops moving it is very likely that it is frozen or dead. In regards to the right and left, each accuses the other of being stuck in old philosophies and incapable of adjusting as our conditions as a nation continually change.

While it can be argued that the "stronger willed" can and /or will prosper, it can be further argued that every human being possesses the potential for greatness. This idea is in line with leftist values, that all people possess potential and so should be provided adequate opportunity to succeed in life. In reference to the individual survival dynamic versus the group survival dynamic, what has to be understood is that Man 'is' simultaneously an island and no island unto himself. One individual can certainly be stronger than another, but such a determination is dependent upon comparison; absent this comparison the strength of the former cannot be validated. The need for comparison for the sake of validation qualifies the group survival dynamic. Further relevance of the group survival dynamic is made clear by the need for networking in social and/or business circles; for what would be the value of a business' product, were there no consumers to purchase it? There is relevance to the Individual survival dynamic as well. A need for a level of selfishness is required in order for an individual's aspirations to be realized, for no man can provide a solution for anyone that he hasn't discovered for himself; but once said aspirations are realized, there is a need for man to share his experiences, for even knowledge or experience absent activity or movement is dead.

The Public's Money

The battle for control over the Public's money forever remains the core purpose of political, business, organized labor and similar organizations. Questions about whether or not money should be spent; or what public dollars should be spent on; or who should do the spending continue to be the topic of debate for campaign after campaign. The right demands more tax relief for businesses, because in their opinion it is the business community that drives our national economy. The left demands adequate services and equal opportunity for the working class and poor, because what would a nation be absent its people?

Today, municipalities across the country are searching for a solution to their financial troubles. What is needed is what I consider to be the only practical solution: adequate education and jobs. I know that it sounds like a political ploy when we hear politicians saying "what we need are jobs, jobs, jobs". Though this continues to be an empty statement on the part of some, it 'is' the solution. Eighty percent of Federal, State and local (government) revenue is generated from the working individual.[2] Understandably, high unemployment translates to a suffering economy. The effects of unemployment are immediately felt in local economies. When unemployment percentages are high the demand for Public Assistance and/or public programming increases. The ability of the unemployed individual to care for himself and his family is severely hindered. Properties and other valuables of unemployed persons could potentially be lost. An increasing demand for Public Assistance as a result of unemployment, coupled with a

depleting tax base results in slowed activity
(death).

As it turns out, what is required is a joining of certain principles on the right and the left; where individuals are empowered through education, workforce development and job opportunity. As the individual becomes more self-sufficient, he transforms from being dependent on public resources to being a contributor and supporter of the same.

In a book that I wrote titled the African American Dilemma I made mention of the times of the hunter-gatherers, where the Men often hunted animals for food in order to feed their families. Over time, increasing inclement weather conditions coupled with a scarcity of animals made hunting for food nearly impossible. The Women of the tribe(s) began to plant seeds for vegetation, eventually producing a surplus of food. This abundance of food (resources) eliminated the "need" for hunting. Consider this for a moment. Equally noticeable was the fact that this abundance of food attracted more people, resulting in over-population.[3] The idea communicated here is that whenever abundance is generated, 'need' is eliminated.

One example that is usually considered a negative is the fact that the appearance of abundance in the way of Public Assistance has reduced or eliminated the need to labor on the part of some citizens. Let's be honest; there are some people who take advantage of Public

Assistance. In their minds, this apparent "free money" has eliminated the need for them to seek employment. This does not apply to all persons on Public Assistance, but certainly some. We must do a better job in determining who actually needs assistance and who's abusing the opportunity for assistance. We need to wean capable individuals off of public assistance, thereby allowing more resources for the people who truly need them.

One example of a positive though, is an increase (abundance) in education and workforce development opportunities, leading to employment. Empowering individuals to be self-sufficient, particularly individuals collecting Public Assistance and individuals re-entering society from the prison system, "reduces the need for public money". Often times the demand for individuals to fend for themselves is contradicted by the unwillingness on the part of some on the right and the left to provide opportunities. Increasing the size of one's workforce leads to increased productivity (if the market demands an increase). An increase in the size of a city's workforce could lead to increased property sales, resulting in increased tax collections. An increase in revenue could eventually mean adequately funded public programs (Education, public safety, healthcare, infrastructure, etc.).

We need to spend our public dollars intelligently. We should spend it on education, workforce development and job creation. We need better support for small businesses, which employs eighty percent of our nation's labor force. [2] Government should create an environment where small businesses have an opportunity to grow or expand; such an expansion will increase labor demands, resulting in more jobs. Furthermore, opportunities for growth help municipalities to retain good employers.

Ladies and Gentlemen of the right, this is not liberal, but is quite conservative. The result of the above action is a reduction of the over-all tax burden for everyone; individuals and businesses alike. Increasing the number of persons contributing to the tax base reduces or eliminates the need to increase taxes. What is required of us is a slight adjustment in our thinking. Our desire for immediate gratification prevents us from possessing the patience necessary to appreciate incremental victories. While the above effort will not produce an immediate influx of extremely large amounts of revenue, it will provide us tax relief over time.

In our efforts to increase revenue and balance the budget, each partisan group needs to give more consideration to the other's position. Only then will we be able to intelligently assess our circumstances and make the type of decisions that will lead our cities and our nation towards prosperity.

2   Business is Business

Municipalities throughout our country are going through very rough times financially, as many of us are currently experiencing in the cities wherein we each reside. Apparently past practices have not been the best, and so today we as government officials, business owners, and constituents are charged with the duty of not only restoring our local economies by reducing wasteful spending publicly (as well as in our personal lives); but we are also charged with the duty of restoring the People's faith and hopefully their participation in government.

So many of us possess feelings of disinterest or indifference when it comes to government; our local governments in particular. We've made the determination that government is simply politics as usual and that neither our vote nor our participation matters much. As a result, many constituents, especially poor families have learned to function "absent government". This disinterest in government exists, despite the fact that contributions towards government operations are continually made by poor persons, particularly through sales tax. By functioning absent government I mean that poor persons and others who might have become fed up with ineffective government have accepted their condition and have come to the conclusion that they "just have to make do" with what they have. For these persons, government doesn't exist. Take into account also the fact that the perception that most people have about government, what government is and what its processes are, are incorrect. Our knowledge about government is inadequate and so 'we fail' in our attempts to make government work for us; all the while assuming that it is 'government' that has failed.

This disconnectedness that exists between government and its constituents has led to consistent frustration and dissatisfaction. Politicians and government representatives express frustration, because of a lack of participation on the part of voters and constituents. Constituents express frustration and dissatisfaction with what they deem to be inadequate representation and inadequate services on the part of government.

As taxpaying citizens we cannot afford to become disconnected from our government. Dissatisfaction with government should not cause one to merely write government off, but should instead fuel the individual with the determination to demand acceptable representation from those whom we empower to work in our service. If I could make one suggestion to the taxpayer it would be this:

"Demand a return on investment."

While many may frown at the idea of government being business, it 'is' a business essentially. If we were to compare a city to a trust organization it would go as follows: a City or trust operates like a business, characterized by consistent investments made by the taxpayers (who for these purposes we will call shareholders) into a municipality (a Trust). This "Trust" is managed by a Mayor (Trust manager), with oversight from a City Council (Board of Trustees). The duties of this elected body are thus: to manage the assets of the shareholders for the shareholders benefit. If we imagined a city to be one large building within which this business trust operated; the public works and water departments would qualify as the maintenance crew, charged with the responsibility of keeping the building clean and functional, and the police department is obviously security. Cities have accounting departments, legal departments, personnel departments, etc. just as any other business does. If it walks and talks like a business, chances are it is a business. In the business of government we <u>sell</u> services. Constituents must understand this point in order to know how to take full advantage of the services that government has to offer.

Each of us as taxpayers, from the most poor to the wealthiest, make contributions towards this Trust; and we put "our trust" in the persons that we elect to manage our assets and to make the best possible investments on our behalf. As with any business, contributors expect a return on their investment; and not just a return, but a better than decent return. If the contributors feel as if they are being short-changed, misled or taken for granted, they normally seek recourse via the Board of Trustees, or even the court system. In this particular instance, we as contributing shareholders or tax-paying constituents seek recourse through the voting booths during elections.

As voting and contributing members to this municipal organization we have to be sure that we not only choose or elect the best possible persons for the job, but we must also make sure that those who we choose to represent us are providing us the best possible services that our tax dollars could buy. Everything from snow removal to trash collection to police protection to quality education in our public schools to economic development to street or infrastructure improvements is the short list of what our tax dollars pay for. Residents in low income communities have become accustomed to mediocrity; where cracked sidewalks, dilapidated housing and criminal activity has become acceptable. On the contrary, our tax dollars should assure us improve sidewalks, respectable housing stock and adequate police protection to sustain the quality of life that we each deserve.

My intent here is not to suggest picket lines or protest outside of city hall, but instead to suggest active, intelligent participation in your government. In addition, it is my intention to reaffirm what each of you should already know; YOU SHOULD ALWAYS REMAIN IN TUNE WITH,

AND FOLLOW YOUR INVESTMENT. If I were to collect $500 from you for the purpose of making an investment on your behalf, I am pretty sure that you would follow up with me regularly to assure that your money was being invested wisely. Yet, you spend thousands of dollars annually investing into our system of government and never think to ask your representatives about how your money is being used. Who walks into a department store, puts their money on the cashier's counter and then walks out of the store without receiving services or a product?

We cannot allow the caretakers of our assets off of the hook. We must remind our caretakers that we expect better than good service; that we expect the intelligent investment of our assets into good public programs, i.e. public education, workforce development initiatives leading to job creation for city residents and opportunity for local small businesses and businesses in general. We must demand adequate response(s) from our service providers. We do not have to be antagonistic or approach our representatives in anger or frustration; we simply need to ask those very relevant questions regarding government services. Anything short of the aforementioned would simply be bad (for) business. We need to keep our elected officials to task to be sure that they are making good decisions that will improve our financial health, and overall quality of life.

3   Middle Ground

What is becoming more and more apparent as time progresses is the need for government and private industry to partner or work together to prevent our cities and our nation from falling further into financial ruin. Practices over many years past have led our government and therefore our people near the brink of pauperism (poverty); so much so that cities around our nation have become heavily dependent on state and federal resources. It is as if the minds managing government have become conditioned into patterns of service absent ideas and efforts towards revenue generation. There is no individual household or any business that can survive when its expenses supersede its income.

Statements like the one mentioned above usually

send some constituents into a rage. The idea of government functioning as (a) business or the idea of government being in any way preoccupied with revenue generation somehow causes many to think that government has its priorities mixed up. Nothing could be further from the truth. What must be understood by constituents is that if government fails to generate revenue it will not be able to provide the type of services that we the constituents demand. We as constituents have to be clear about what is required in order for government to be efficient in its providing of services. Government employees have to be paid; materials have to be purchased; services that are beyond government's ability lawfully or otherwise have to be purchased; in most cases

from the private sector. All of this and the many, many things not mentioned here are required in order for government to operate effectively. It may come across as harsh (though to be harsh is not my intent) but government does not operate on votes alone. It takes revenue; and it is our responsibility as voting and taxpaying members of our various cities to assure that we elect the persons who we 'believe' can provide deliverables. It is just as important that we, the members of our various cities remove those elected persons with whom we've become dissatisfied; not because they didn't return our phone call, or because they did not attend our neighborhood meeting; but because they might not have made a respectable effort to make

government better for the people. We need to be
absolutely honest with ourselves and with others
when making such a determination.

A major cause of increasing deficits in our cities, specifically within the state of New York is the increasing cost of healthcare and pension programs. In a strange way it is a little comical that government never considered the possibility that people might become healthier and live longer. Nevertheless people 'are' living longer and so in some cities there is just as much money being spent on retired persons, as there is being spent on persons who are actively working. As we can see some government regulation even hurts government. In the state of New York existing residency laws on the state level further hinders our cities' abilities (upstate New York cities specifically) to generate revenue; particularly as it relates to Police Department employees. Today, the federal and state governments are calling on cities to be more self-sustaining; but some state mandates, which obligate municipalities to perform and manage certain programs or services, have allowed a slow deterioration our cities' financial health through these very programs and services that we have been obligated to perform. Though efforts to provide mandate relief are underway, there are remaining (state) restrictions that could use some fine tuning. The continual implementation of incentive regulations is one method through which federal, state and even local governments could pull back on possibly obsolete regulatory methods, while simultaneously implementing intelligent performance and / or similar metrics to assure that we are reaching goals that are satisfying to the taxpayers. For those who may be unfamiliar with the term(s), incentive regulation is a method used to overcome information or communication problems. It is the use of rewards or penalties to cause a business to reach desired goals where the business is afforded some discretion in reaching said goals.[5] This idea or method is based on a psychological concept called Operant Conditioning; where penalties or rewards are used to generate a desired conditioned response. [1]

Though existing government regulations continue to make it tough for municipalities to become self-sustaining, representatives in city government continue in their efforts to generate revenues at home. In most struggling cities, unemployment is ground zero. Unfortunately, government, or the public sector in general, cannot hire everyone. The reduction of our unemployment percentage is a responsibility that both the public and private sector share (or at least should share). Cities across the country are making efforts to improve their infrastructure, housing stock, and business corridors. Efforts are continually made to attract young, creative, enterprising professionals to populate developing urban cores; all the while there remain unskilled, unemployed persons who are native to these cities. In many cities around our country there are young adults and adults in general who desire work opportunities; but who may not possess the skill sets that some work opportunities require. In the spirit of right-winged philosophy we could very easily remove ourselves from the responsibility of caring for our fellow man by saying that those persons who are unskilled as a result of an incomplete education or those persons who might be behind the times in regards to know how, skills and abilities due to incarceration are the creators of their own fate, and so have to live with their choices. To those of the right-wing I say to you, this is true; but who do you think will be covering the cost when said persons look to the various social services departments for relief or assistance; or when persons re-entering society from prison return back to a life of crime, ultimately returning back to prison? It cost tax payers in Onondaga County (NY) over $400 per night to house an individual in the Onondaga County Justice Center. It would make more sense and be more cost effective to provide at risk individuals work opportunities that could result in a person 'earning' $400 per week. Obviously it is not my intent to "guilt" businesses into doing anything. It is also not my intent to make excuses for persons **who repeatedly make unintelligent choices**. What I am attempting to do here is appeal to your logic. Being the business minds that you are I would think that the numbers would make sense. Increasing financial hardships are causing more and more people to become dependent on public assistance. This results in a greater expense for each and every one of us. If it is tax relief that we desire, the solution is very simple: we must work to reduce or eliminate 'the need' for public money. The illusion that we taxpayers and/or business owners are alone on our own island(s) is contradicted by the demand on us to cover the cost for those who may be unable to fend for themselves.

Government should not have to implement regulations on businesses to strengthen the financial health of our cities. Underdeveloped neighborhoods, moderate to high levels of criminal activity, high property taxes, decreased population density; these are some of the major

deterrents to investment. A reduction or
elimination of these types of deterrents
improves the quality of the environment. Such
an improvement is great for business.

Government should lead the charge in the effort
to improve the financial health of our cities by
investing in work force development initiatives.
More effective programming should be
developed to wean able bodied persons off of
public assistance. A greater effort should be
made to assure that returning unemployed
veterans have access to education and work
opportunities. If 80% of local, state and federal
revenue is generated via the working
individual,[2] government needs to consistently
and relentlessly spend its energy and resources

on educating, training, and empowering its citizens. This is an intelligent investment.

The private sector, in an effort to secure a quality business and/or work environment for its employees, partners and consumers, and to reduce its tax burden and similar expenses should willingly assist government and the public sector in the effort to educate, train and employ its citizens. If I and four other persons lived in the same house where as a group we shared the expenses, our individual contributions might be at a level that each of us could easily bear; but should four of us become unemployed, the entire cost of living for all five occupants would fall on the one remaining employed individual. People, this is easy math.

Currently in the city of Syracuse more than 50% of the assessable land is nontaxable. Add to that, a large amount of tax delinquent properties, and it may not be unreasonable to assume that we may be dangerously approaching or passing a situation where more than 60% of our city's assessable properties generates "zero" dollars in revenue. Keep in mind that while the first greatest revenue generator for government is the working individual, the second greatest revenue generator for municipalities in particular, is its land resources.[2]

In summary, we need effective public / private partnerships if we are to ever revitalize our cities; but it cannot be a partnership "in name only". It has to be a true partnership, characterized by a shared burden and/or a real exchange. Education and workforce development programs are an intelligent use of public money. We can, as municipalities, continue to do "spot development" in an attempt to attract new talent to our cities. We can continue to contract with non-local businesses or businesses that are not anchored within our cities' limits, with no local hiring requirements. We can continue to improve our appearances in an effort to attract new business investments; but all of this is for naught when we fail to invest in those persons who are native to our cities and who are willing to work; poor persons, laborers, and small business owners who remain loyal and who, despite our neglect, still chooses to call our cities home. To the business community: you are doing us absolutely **no favors** by simply taking up space and taken advantage of our tax incentives, if unemployed persons living within our cities are not provided at the very least training or work 'opportunities' within your business. This is not a demand for the unreasonable, but instead an appeal for what you cannot deny is reasonable. To government: while it may not sound sexy, we need to seek a return on investment, namely job opportunities for persons who reside within the boundaries of our municipalities. We cannot continue to cater to businesses that choose not to appreciate our circumstances and our needs as a city; businesses that continuously collect money at the expense of our taxpayers and take and spend it elsewhere. We need both

businesses and government to "buy into" this
idea of a shared responsibility. There should be
a "purposeful" effort on the part of the public
and private sector to improve our cities' financial
health; thereby securing both the business' and
our cities' future.

4   To Our Public Partners

The ending of the previous chapter is a perfect segue into a part of this discussion that will certainly ruffle some feathers. In what I believe was a sincere effort on the part of government to be of great service to its constituents, government partnered with various members of our communities through non-profit organizations. Essentially government partnerships with nonprofits were established to provide services for residents that government did not or could not provide. If the reader would refer back to the comparison made to the hunter-gatherers in the first chapter, the reason for what I'm about to say may become clear. ***An increase in or an abundance of resources of any*** *type causes the elimination of need in many respects.* The providing of government resources in the name of human services has attracted the attention of, not only those who are sincerely in need of said services, but also those more able bodies who view these services as an opportunity to acquire resources with little to no effort. I find it necessary to reiterate that during the times of the hunter–gatherers the abundance of food resources led to overpopulation. *People concentrate or attract to where ever there appears to be an abundance of resources*. In regards to human services, the overpopulation of the offices of the various providers of human services led the providers of these services to demand more assistance from government. The appearance of increased demand for services caused government to pump more money into human services. People, let's be clear about what is happening here. The ease by which some individuals have acquired resources has eliminated in these individuals "the need" to make an effort to learn, to work, and in some cases, to even think. The previous statement is not in any way a negative judgment against persons who may sincerely need assistance as a result of unexpected unemployment, mental or physical disabilities, or simply because said person has fallen upon hard times. It is most certainly though, a judgment against those who have and/or continue to take the availability of these resources for granted. What is interesting is this: an able-bodied person, who saw an easy opportunity and took advantage of said opportunity under false pretenses, has now in fact 'made herself' incapable via a lack of effort and a lack of education. As a result, this individual is not as 'hirable' as a more skilled person would be. Think about it; she is now legitimately dependant on public assistance. Her inactivity has made it such that her initial fraudulent inability to provide for herself has now become an actual inability to provide for herself; go figure. Though right-winged philosophy is questionable at times, they are right about one thing: nonstop spending in the name of human services as a result of "an appearance" of increased demand over the years has played a major part in the severe weakening of the financial health of our cities, our states and our nation. Republicans and

Democrats alike, we cannot improve ourselves if
we do not first admit our problems.

Individuals were not the only ones who saw easy
opportunity and took advantage. Even some
nonprofit organizations saw an opportunity to
take advantage of governments' generosity. In
the city of Syracuse nonprofit organizations pop
up like bugs in the summer. A business mind
understands that need or demand translates
into a potential new market, and eventually,
profit. Nonprofit organizations often recognize
need, and as a result they seek to satisfy the
need for no other purpose than to attract more
money from government and/or other funding
institutions. Usually the employees of these

nonprofit organizations are in no way in touch with the community that they are expected to serve. This disconnect on the part of the nonprofit organization is the reason why so many of their efforts fail. These 'for profit efforts' masquerading as nonprofits lie about their abilities, cook their books and fabricate their numbers in an effort to attract more money from government. These nonprofit organizations ventures into areas of service where they have absolutely no experience. I would be an absolute insincere, dishonest coward if I did not make clear the fact that some of these nonprofits to which I am referring are churches. This is not a slam to all churches or nonprofits. There are some nonprofits and churches that do great work in our cities; some of them even pay property taxes. But for the many nontaxable organizations who consistently seek financial support from our governments, but who in turn provide absolutely nothing in the way of service agreements, job training and work opportunity in conjunction with community investment; shame on you.

Government needs to demand more of its nonprofit institutions. Nonprofit organizations that do not pay property taxes must be cognizant of the damage they do to our second greatest revenue generator, i.e. our land resources. Since by state or federal law some nonprofits are not obligated to pay taxes, a nonprofits aspirations to expand and occupy more land should be matched by a willingness to offer education, training and work opportunities for a designated number of persons residing in their respective cities; not as a result of forced regulations, but because it is the will of the nonprofit to make an intelligent investment into the community that surrounds it. Or, maybe government should look into establishing a 'purchasing cap', which would prevent a single nonprofit organization from purchasing beyond a designated number of acres in order to maintain a respectable tax-base.

To the tax contributors and elected officials who represent them: we can no longer allow ourselves to be bullied by special interests from the right or the left at the expense of the whole. Keep in mind that business, like man is

simultaneously an island and no island unto
itself. The services provided by the nonprofit
organizations throughout our cities are certainly
appreciated; but there are certain nonprofits
whose services are not free. We the residents of
the various cities throughout this nation pay you
for your services. You pay no property taxes; you
do minimal local hiring; you don't pay for our
police, fire or other services. We, the taxpayers
are not only paying 'you' for your services; we
also pay for police, fire and other services that
you receive from our cities. Essentially, we carry
just about your entire tax burden(s). You literally
drain our local economies.

We need better partnerships where there is a
more balanced give and take. We need our

elected officials at the state and federal level to empower municipalities with the ability to negotiate better deals with these non-profit organizations on behalf of its constituents. State and federal legislators should consider passing laws that obligate these tax-base-eating nonprofits, which have become financial burdens to taxpayers, to pay impact fees or to enter service agreements with the municipalities wherein they conduct business, in an effort offset lost property taxes. To allow this kind of vampirism to continue will assure the absolute destruction of our cities. The future of our cities depends on it. Our financial stability will not be realized otherwise.

5   On the Level

One of the biggest controversies in politics and government concerns corporate influence on the same. Right and left winged Electeds alike receives monetary support from big businesses; especially in state and federal elections. The US Supreme Court's recent support of Super Political Action Committees or Super PACS has elevated the battle for influence over government to an all new level. Super PACS allows for special interests groups, political parties, labor unions, and even elected officials to raise unlimited amounts of money that could essentially be donated in support of a political campaign, against a political campaign or in support or against legislative issues. The one caveat is that the money raised by a Super PAC cannot be given directly to a candidate or to a candidate's campaign; but the money raised by a Super PAC can be spent <u>on behalf</u> of a candidate's campaign. Ultimately a candidate who is backed by a Super PAC may have an unlimited amount of financial resources at his or her disposal, which could strengthen the candidates marketing, advertising and promotional campaign to such a degree that an opponent with less financial support could almost never compete.

The above-mentioned Supreme Court decision has caused a firestorm of protest by citizens groups and similar organizations throughout the nation regarding what these groups consider to be an unfair opportunity for business to gain an even greater leverage over government than actual voting citizens. The average working person who makes minimum wage and who is a taxpaying citizen has issues and concerns that will more than likely never be heard; certainly not to the level of a Corporation possessing large amounts of money set aside specifically for its own political agenda(s). Concerns about decaying housing stock, failing schools, suffering neighborhood business districts and unemployment takes a backseat to extremely well advertised and promoted corporate concerns. This sort of David and Goliath type of story has resulted in an effort to change how political campaigns can be funded. The push for campaign finance reform via public financing has become a major topic of discussion amongst legislative bodies around the country; but what is public financing? Often there are discussions surrounding politics and government that the average voting and even nonvoting citizens are unfamiliar with. There have been different suggestions about how to make the financing of elections fairer to voting citizens. One example of a recommendation for campaign finance reform that I've come across suggest that a new public financing rule could require a candidate for political office to only raise money within the district where the candidate is seeking to be seated. This means that the candidate would not receive any money from persons or corporations located outside of his or her respective district. Another idea for campaign finance reform even suggests that a candidate should only be able to raise money from the voters living within his or her respective district. If either the above were to happen, corporate contributions towards political campaigns would be greatly reduce; even eliminated in some districts.

Understandably the passing of legislation that would require public financing for political campaigns would drive the business community insane. As an elected official I am very pro-business; but there is logic behind public financing that must be understood by the voters. Using the abovementioned examples, candidates seeking public office, if required to raise money from within the districts where they are seeking to be seated, could very well be limited in the amount of corporate money that they could acquire. In this instance, the candidate might have to try to raise money from the average voting citizen within the district. Now, you really have to consider this for a moment; in order to raise money from voters within a respective district, a candidate would most certainly have to go door to door in an effort to establish a relationship with the voter. Let's be clear about what this means. It is not just a matter of a candidate going to a stranger's door and asking for her vote in the coming election; the candidate is going much further by asking the voter to reach into her pocket and to give her hard earned money towards his campaign for office. Herein lays the logic; if a voter is so touched by a candidate's presentation that she reaches into her pocket to gives her hard-earned money towards this candidate's campaign, it is almost very likely that this voter will cast her vote for said candidate. To further clarify: a requirement to raise campaign funds from the voters within a district where one is seeking to be seated allows for a candidate to not only raise campaign money, but also secure what might very well be guaranteed votes. An effort like this one could definitely level the playing field making the average voter as influential on government as a Corporation within the same district. The obvious benefit of corporate contributions is the ability to pay for an effective marketing campaign. With public financing (little to no corporate contributions), the candidate would have to work much harder to build a presence amongst voters. If each candidate had to work just as hard as his or her opponent to raise money, particularly from the voters, political races would be much more competitive. Consider this.

In addition to leveling the playing field, public financing could lead to increased voter participation. Voters who have lost faith in government and even nonvoters might be motivated to participate if it is learned that corporate influence over elected persons has been greatly decreased as a result of campaign finance reform. I believe it also safe to say that such reform would allow for elected persons to vote their conscience, absent a potential penalty of reduced campaign financing from corporate contributors.

Public financing would certainly change a lot about politics and government; but it must be remembered that corporations as legal persons are constituents as well, and so must be represented by government. In my opinion the balancing or leveling of the playing field does not decrease the value of corporate contributions to political campaigns; it simply makes the process more competitive. Leveling the playing field makes the candidate and/or elected official more honest, and in the end, the constituents win. This is but one way of returning government back to the People. Being an elected official, I seek to raise campaign funds via the business community and the average voting citizen. Corporate interests must be considered to demonstrate that our cities / states are open for business; but corporations should be good partners and return the favor by training and hiring citizens residing within or near their respective areas. I would like the reader to understand that my repeating of our need for education, workforce development and/or job training, and job opportunities is not an error. I have been and will continue to be purposefully redundant in an effort to drive the message home.

Equal representation under the law is the right all persons, actual or artificial. If it is truly the desire of our representatives in government to

returned the power of government back to the
people, public financing might have to receive
some serious consideration.

6   Power to the People

If I were to ask the average voter or even the average elected official, "what political seat would you consider to be the most influential or the most powerful?" The immediate reply would most obviously be the President of the United States. Of course I would agree. If I were to ask which elected official would you consider the most influential amongst voters, the answer would probably be the same; or one might reply by saying a US Senator or a US congressman. Certainly due to the amount of media coverage that an elected official on the federal level might receive, said officials' name recognition would be greater than say, a local elected. I would argue though that a pretty influential, if not the most influential elected official (on the voters) would be the local elected.

There is often an argument made that says that politics are local and not national; that all political campaigns start and end with the average voter who resides in small city USA. The local elected is a person just like you and I, who might have grown up in the same circumstances as you and I; he is a person who understands our issues to the core, because our issues are his issue. The local elected either walks or drives the same streets that we walk and drive every single day. She shops at the same grocery stores; her child attends the same schools that our children attend. The local elected uses the same post offices or sits to eat at the same restaurants as you and I; and because this local elected is just like you or just like me, he understands our needs or the needs of our neighborhoods. He truly has his finger on the pulse of the community.

If an individual who was of a select community at some point in her life becomes the choice of the people to act as their representative in government; and if this individual over the years have performed to the satisfaction of those who elected her to office, it is not unreasonable to assume that she might have developed a major influence on her constituents; not as a result of manipulation, but because her constituents trust her. In this type of scenario this local elected would become a very, very important person to any candidate seeking to be elected to some higher office, and requiring votes from her district. This local elected essentially becomes a tool for her constituents, for she will assure that the issues of her constituency are heard by the individuals seeking higher government offices. In other words, a local elected, through the power and support of her constituency could affect the direction of elections on the county, state, and federal levels.

Within municipal governments there exist legislative or lawmaking bodies that are similar to the lawmaking bodies on the state and federal levels. There are some cities where these lawmaking bodies are made up of Councilors. Councilors are usually the political representatives for specific Council districts within the municipality. There are also some Councilors who represent an entire city. There are some cities though that are broken up into wards and these wards are represented by Ward bosses and/or Aldermen. In most cities, Council districts are larger than wards; in fact in cities like Syracuse New York, the Council districts are made up of a certain number of wards. Most cities operate with one legislative branch of government; meaning the city either has a city Council made up of Councilors or a city Council made up of Aldermen. Keep in mind that Councilors represent Council districts and Aldermen represent wards.

I often wonder why cities only have one legislative branch of government. Considering that cities have Council districts which are made up of Ward districts, why not have both Councilors and Aldermen? Consider the scenario discussed a little earlier in this chapter regarding local Electeds who are chosen from amongst the people they are to represent. In fact, let's consider a Council district that I used to represent. I, at one point, represent the fourth Council district in the city of Syracuse. The 4th Council district was made up of eleven wards at that time. In each ward there is a Ward committee that is managed by a Ward chair. This Ward chair position 'could be' synonymous with that of a Ward boss and/or an Alderman. In fact, though it has become a common practice in most municipalities for political party bosses to appoint these Ward Chairs, persons living within a select Ward can actually campaign and challenge a sitting Ward Chair for his or her position. That's right; I am saying that a Ward Chair is essentially an elected position. The charter for the city of Syracuse only allows for a Mayor and Council form of government; but imagine how much more responsive city government would be if the people elected both Councilors and Aldermen. As a city Councilor I work pretty close with my constituency; but I do not work as close with my constituency as the various Ward Chairs do. These individuals have an even greater understanding of the needs of their respective wards. It is my opinion that if the city had two legislative branches of government; one being made up of district Councilors; the other being made up of Ward Chairs or Aldermen; there is a greater chance that government would act in accordance to the will of the people.

These Ward Chairs or Aldermen are the ambassadors or community brokers who know and understand the will of the people. There is seldom any elected official in municipal government that is closer to a given Ward's constituents. This is another way in which government could be given back to the people. Reestablishing Aldermen to represent the various wards within a Council district opens up government to the people in a way in which it hasn't been for decades. An Alderman has the ability to touch people more directly and more often than any other elected in municipal government. Such a close connection with constituents would more than likely increase the level of constituent participation in government. The People might feel more inclined to participate, because the person from down the street, whom they see almost every day, is their representative. Reenacting an Aldermen Council might also inspire voters to consider a run for public office at some point in their futures. Aldermen could eventually move on to become District Councilors, at-large Councilors and even Mayors. This would truly be a government for the people and by the people.

There is though a problem with this idea. In some cities where Aldermen have been reduced to mere Ward Chairs, the idea of resurrecting Aldermen is a danger to the status quo. The ability of political party bosses to appoint Ward committee chairs allows these bosses to control the nomination processes, and thereby influence elections. Ultimately, these political party bosses control government through the people that they appoint/elect. In many instances the People are manipulated into voting for persons who they otherwise might not have voted for. The People are caused to vote for persons who are in no way connected to their respective issues; thus the people are dissatisfied with the representation.

If local government would consider establishing
two legislative bodies that would speak on
behalf of its people, the people would then have
a greater voice; and increase participation is
almost assured. Having both an Alderman and a
Councilor would allow opportunities for the
Alderman to, not only lobby the Councilor, but
bring issues of the community that he
represents to the floor himself. Here we would
see a true balance of power between the
legislative and executive bodies; a government
where those elected are truly in touch with the
concerns of its constituents; a government that
would truly be responsive to its people.

7   Vote for Change

I would like to take this opportunity to restate for the reader the clinical definition for insanity. The clinical definition for insanity is to do the same thing over and over again and each time expecting a different result. What can we say about the person who either has never participated in politics and/or government; or the person who, as a result of frustration, has chosen to no longer participate? Here is what should be considered: though the individual in both instances fails to participate in the process, she expresses dissatisfaction with the fact that her circumstances or the circumstances in her neighborhood never seems to improve. You be the judge in determining whether such behavior can be qualified as insane. While this person's frustration may very well be warranted, being frustrated and inactive does not solve the problem. It would be more to this person's benefit to use said frustration as motivation to evoke change. Otherwise, complaints absent action are moot.

The example mentioned above is very familiar to most of us. We often hear the complaints amongst our peers throughout our communities. We hear complaints about inadequate services on the part of the police departments, the public works departments, etc., and in the same breath the complainers go on to say "that is exactly why I cannot be bothered with politics and government". There are people living within our communities who believe that by not participating, they are somehow 'hurting government'. This idea is equivalent to saying "I am dissatisfied with my house, and so I will no longer invest any energy into its maintenance and the like, and I could care less about what happens to my house." Now we all know what's going to happen. If I decide to no longer invest in the maintenance of my house, eventually my house will cave in on top of me. In respect to government, our decision to not give attention to government will only result in our further dissatisfaction with the same. In the end, "we" are the ones who end up hurting; not government. Government departments do carry out routine responsibilities, but in most instances (unfortunately) government services are complaint driven. Government service providers do not ride around looking for problems (well, not most of them); that would be a waste of taxpayer dollars. Our service providers need our assistance in identifying problems that require our attention. When there is an issue in our neighborhoods that we feel need government's attention, we must make some noise in order to attract said attention. Municipalities are made up of miles and miles of sidewalks, roads and green spaces; and there are a lot more citizens than there are government workers. Government workers cannot and will not see everything. We, the citizens, have to help them out by letting them know what and where the problems are.

Within the process of government, if there is a problem that requires a department to spend money, said department must receive the permission of the administration and the legislative body. There are some constituents who believe that the departments or the administration can just change policy or spend money willy-nilly. This is not true. Efforts that require spending or changes in policy must be presented to the legislative body for its approval, and then must be signed by the executive office, namely the Mayor, Governor, or President.

My reason for the above discussion is twofold: 1) it is my opinion that government is responsible for educating its citizens about its processes.

Such an education will eliminate a lot of confusion about government operations; and 2) to demonstrate the importance of constituent participation. If we as constituents are not reaching out to government and calling government's attention to our concerns, government "will fail" or at least we as constituents will think it failed in its efforts to be responsive.

Each of us as taxpaying citizens has issues for which we need answers or assistance. For those of us who are registered voters, we participate or at least should participate in the election process to choose a person who we believe will provide us her or his best effort to be responsive to our needs. When we have honestly come to the conclusion that the person who we voted for has failed to provide us deliverables, we seek to replace said person with another, with the hopes that this next person will do better.

Communities of color historically have the lowest amount of voter participation; and so understandably the areas inhabited by communities of color tend to be underdeveloped. Certainly there are some who will argue that the level of (voter) participation should not matter; that it is the duty of government to provide services for every single person residing within its jurisdiction. I agree with this assertion; but what business or what household runs on autopilot? Within a given municipality, certain neighborhoods receive an abundance of attention, because the inhabitants of said neighborhoods continually demands attention. If communities of color and/or low income communities increased their participation in the political process, I guarantee that they will begin to receive the long-overdue attention that they deserve. The time of mere complaining, absent action has to come to an end. There is absolutely no way that as a taxpaying citizen I would be satisfied with unplowed streets or absentee landlords or disturbances of any sort that would negatively impact my quality of life. The citizens must be educated, reeducated and/or re-acclimated in government operations. The citizens must be empowered with information so that they may understand how to use government effectively.

When, as a result of inadequate government services, the people have lost their way, it is the responsibility of government to bring the People back and restore the People's faith in government.

To the Citizens: Let us become more educated about government so that we will no longer feel hoodwinked by our Electeds. A very good friend of mines always says that a card shark is no longer a card shark when you can understand his game; your understanding his game forces him to play the game honestly (well, at least he'll play the game honestly with you). Let us understand the condition of our cities and also understand what is truly required to improve them, and thereby empower ourselves to see through the manipulation, exaggerations and dishonesty. Let us no longer get caught up in the whirlwind of political agendas that are not sincerely pushed for "our" purposes, but instead at our expense. Let us be absolutely clear that positive change does not happen absent effort. We cannot sit idly by and expect government to work for us automatically. Each and every one of us has to be responsible participants. We must do our part to make sure that our respective corner of the world is receiving the attention it deserves. We must participate in our government; we must participate in elections (especially local elections); we must vote if we want change. To do anything less while simultaneously expecting more is absolutely insane.

In the End

There is so much that could be said about government's inadequacy, or the lack of participation on the part of the People. There is a tendency within our society to pawn the responsibility for our circumstances off onto the next guy or the next governing body. Very seldom in politics, government, and community or even in our personal lives do we take ownership of and responsibility for our conditions; despite the fact that we each exercise our freedom to choose in every instant. Even when circumstances are beyond our control, it is up to us to decide how to respond to said circumstances. We have become so conditioned, that when a person tells us the truth about our condition, we feel offended and get upset, despite the fact that we know that our condition is a bad one. Certainly any disruption to our established routine behaviors would be quite unsettling. We really need to SNAP out of it.

The self determinism of Republican conservatives and the sometimes self-righteousness of Democratic liberals, Green Party supporters etc. creates the type of extremes in ideas and actions that inevitably leads to an imbalance, so disruptive that it seems nearly impossible for us to recover. Under the auspices of constituent services, politicians from the left and the right jockey for position for no other purpose than to establish their (personal) significance or to promote their specific issues at the taxpayer's expense. At their various extremes political parties around the country are so preoccupied with their own ideas that the actual cause(s) of our troubles and the actual solution(s) for the same (troubles) escape them.

Constituents, in their own self-righteousness, approach elected officials with the most ridiculous hostility; some of which is warranted; most of which is exaggerated; and this they do with absolute disregard for any other community. Self-determinism if not properly managed can be very dangerous. Playing the part of savior for all things if not properly managed can also be very dangerous.

When considered objectively, most of us would agree that these types of behaviors are very destructive; we would especially agree if and when said behaviors are displayed by "the opposing person/party".

There is definitely a lot of hypocrisy within government; but there is just as much hypocrisy amongst constituents. Add to this the often misleading reporting on the part of some news media and our condition as a society, which unfortunately seems to be characterized by ignorance, confusion, intolerance and selfishness, is understood. Nobody seems to ever want to compromise.

Some may not wish to acknowledge what I have just said; and some will certainly be offended; but it doesn't change the fact that the above statement is true. Political correctness makes

sense, except when it is maintained at the
expense of our government and its people.

The title of this book, "Necessary Adjustments", suggests the need for each and every one of us to give all matters, all ideas, and all circumstances 'due consideration' before passing judgment or coming to a conclusion; for absent such consideration, no truly intelligent determination can or will be made.

The Author

Khalid Bey is a lifetime resident of the City of Syracuse. He is a graduate of the public school system; and currently he is a proud City Councilor for the People of the City of Syracuse, New York. As an active community member for over 22 years and an employee within government for several years now, Khalid is well aware of what is required for effective governing. In his time as a City Councilor and as the Chairman of the Committee for Economic Development, Downtown & Metropolitan Planning, Khalid has been at the forefront of the battle for job opportunities for city residents, fair and respectable housing and safer neighborhoods.

With an educational background in the Social Sciences, Khalid continues to use his talents an author and a public speaker. He has lectured at a number of colleges and universities, as well as a number of community events along the East coast and in the Midwest, speaking particularly about man's personal identity, human behavior and human relationships. He now adds the subject of good governing to his portfolio.

An author of eight (8) published books, Khalid Bey clearly has a lot to offer. Stating his recent realization of his passion for empowering others, Khalid Bey says "who would imagine that empowering others and seeing others do well could be so satisfying". As a City Councilor,

Khalid Bey takes advantage of the opportunity to fulfill his passion to make the lives of others better. His works continues to win favor with readers. When ask what it is that he aspires to do more than all else, he replied "to understand and inspire".

Khalid is a proud Democrat, having been involved with the Onondaga County (New York) Democratic Party for several years now. As a former Regional Coordinator for the New York State Senate's Democratic Conference, the experience and relationships that Khalid has accumulated on the State and Federal level have proven to be invaluable to him as a local legislator. Currently, he is the Chairman of his City's Democratic 18th Ward Committee.

Khalid's passion to empower people, neighborhoods, and communities, continue to be the driving force behind his efforts as a representative.

In addition to writing books, speaking publicly and volunteering throughout the Syracuse community, Khalid manages a small business of the south side of the City.

An insightful Man, Khalid lives by his coined slogan, "In order to change the world, all one has to do is change his mind".

Be on the lookout for much more from this inspiring author.

Bibliography

- [1] Introduction to Psychology: Gateways to Mind and Behavior (11th Ed.), by Dennis Coon and John O. Mitterer. Thompson/Wadsworth. United States.

- [2] The Craft of Public Administration (9th Ed.), by George Berkley and John Rouse. McGraw/Hill. Boston.

- [3] World Civilizations: The Global Experience. (5th Ed.) By Peter N. Stearns, Michael Adas, Stuart B. Schwartz and Marc Jason Gilbert. Pearson / Longman. New York

- [4] Guns, Germs, and Steel, by Jared Diamond. W. W. Norton & Company. New York.

- [5] Introduction to the Fundamentals of Incentive Regulation, By Sanford V. Berg. Director, Public Utility Research Center. University of Florida.

www.ingramcontent.com/pod-product-compliance
Lightning Source LLC
LaVergne TN
LVHW051603080426
835510LV00020B/3105